THE WORLD

AS

100 PEOPLE

THE W🌍RLD

AS

100 PE⊙PLE

A visual guide to 7 billion humans

ILLUSTRATIONS BY **AILEEN LORD**

**Smith
Street
Books**

INTRODUCTION

The world in which we live is a crowded place. We are the only species to have colonised every continent on the globe, filling the landscape with people as we go. Yet, our world is unbalanced. In the West, it is easy to forget that our privileged lifestyles – with access to jobs, infrastructure, the internet, entertainment, fresh food – do not represent how the rest of the world lives. On a global scale this way of life is, in fact, the minority.

The human race has increased exponentially in the last 200 years. Since 1800, the global population grew from 1 billion to 7 billion by 2011, and is expected to grow by a further 3 billion by 2083, meaning the number of people on this planet will have increased by nearly 1,000 per cent in less than 300 years.

But, what would the world's population look like if it was reduced to 100 people? *The World as 100 People* takes this premise and presents our human population as a small global village. Each person represents 70 million people, which is approximately the population of France.

Pairing statistics from global organisations such as WHO, the United Nations and the CIA with clever and striking infographics, this book demonstrates, with startling and often sobering effect, what the world would look like if it was reduced to this small village. How many people would be displaced, have access to clean drinking water, freedom of speech, sanitation? What is the most commonly spoken language? Which continent is most represented and which religion has the most followers? Read on to discover.

DEMOGRAPHICS

GENETICS

100   people have DNA from Mitochondrial Eve

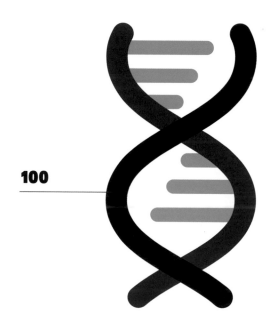

100

OF ALL THE PEOPLE WHO HAVE EVER LIVED

7   people are alive today

93   people have passed away

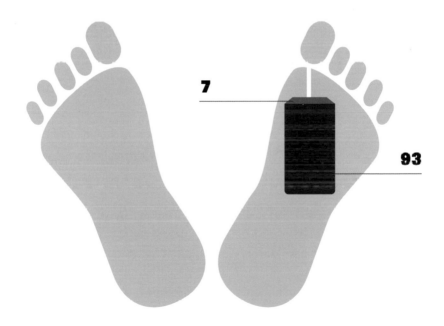

BIRTHS & DEATHS EACH YEAR

2   people will be born

1   person will die

1

2

GENDER

50	people are male
50	people are female

50 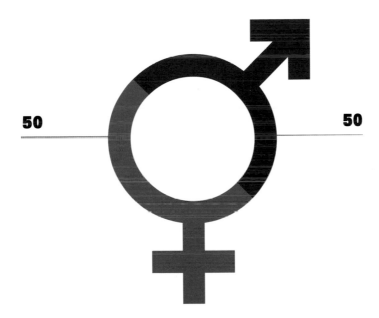 **50**

AGE

26 people are 14 years old or younger
66 people are 15–64 years old
8 people are 65 years old or older

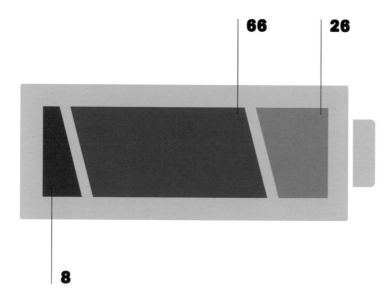

HANDEDNESS

85   people are right-handed

15   people are left-handed

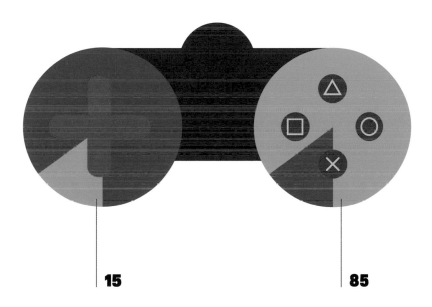

15   **85**

ETHNICITY

61   people are from Asia and the Middle East
19 of whom are from China
18 of whom are from India
4 of whom are from the Middle East

15   people are from Africa
3 of whom are from Nigeria

61

15

9

10 people are from Europe
2 of whom are from Russia

9 people are from South America and the Caribbean
3 of whom are from Brazil

5 people are from North America
4 of whom are from the US

10

5

NAMES

1   person has the surname Li or Lee

1   person has the surname Zhang

1   person has the surname Wang

2   people have the name Muhammed

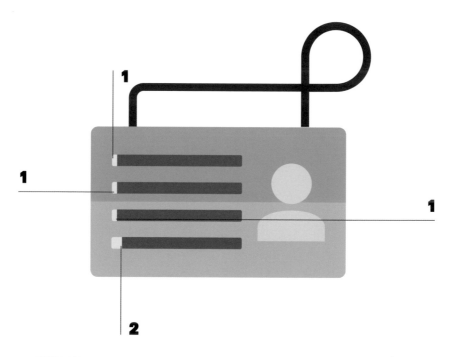

SEXUALITY

90   people are heterosexual

10   people are non-heterosexual

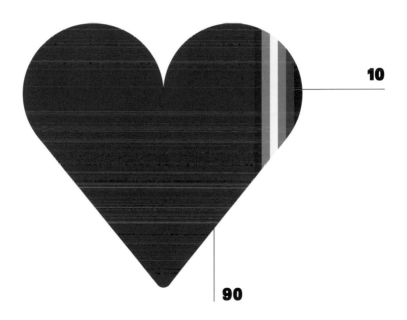

NATIVE LANGUAGES SPOKEN

12   people speak Mandarin Chinese

5   people speak Spanish

5   people speak English

5   people speak Hindi or Bengali

3   people speak Arabic

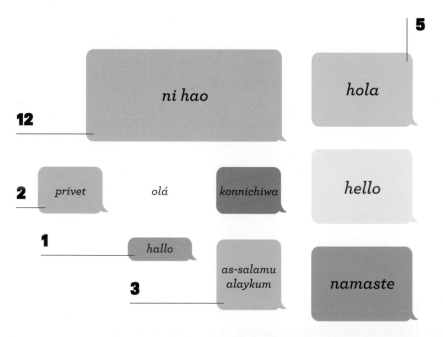

2	people speak Portuguese
2	people speak Russian
2	people speak Japanese
1	person speaks German
63	people speak one of more than 6,000 other languages

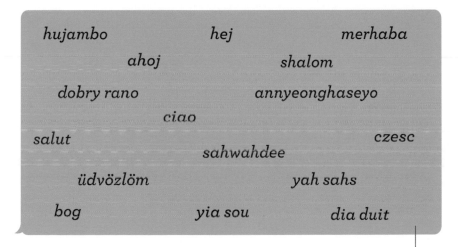

hujambo   hej   merhaba

ahoj   shalom

dobry rano   annyeonghaseyo

ciao

salut   czesc

sahwahdee

üdvözlöm   yah sahs

bog   yia sou   dia duit

63

RELIGION

33   people are Christians

22   people are Muslims

14   people are Hindus

33   **22**   **14**

7   people are Buddhists

2   people are atheists

22   people practise one of more than 4,000 other religions or spiritual traditions

7   **2**   **22**

COASTAL/INLAND

60   people live within 100 kilometres (62 miles) of a coastline

40   people live further inland

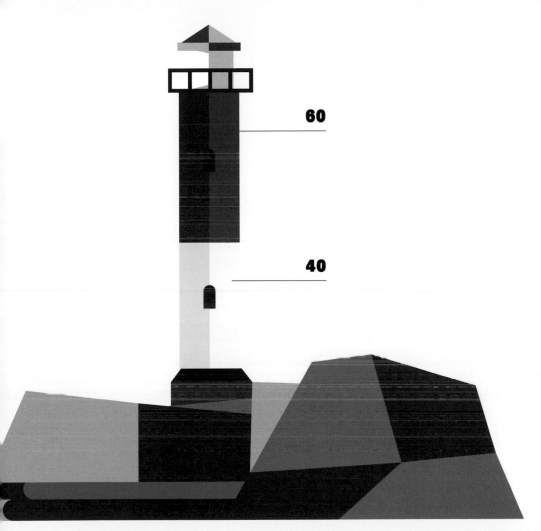

60

40

CITY/COUNTRY

51   people live in an urban area

49   people live in a rural area

51

49

EYE COLOUR

55   people have brown eyes

35   people have hazel eyes

8   people have blue eyes

2   people have green eyes

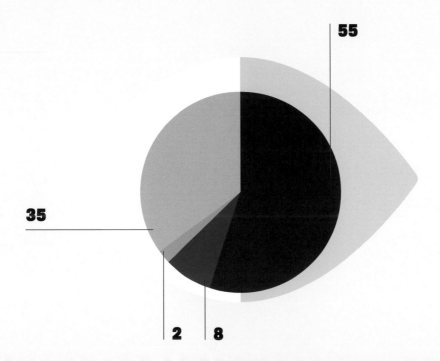

HAIR COLOUR

1	person has red hair
2	people have blond hair
6	people have chestnut hair
7	people have auburn hair
7	people have grey or white hair
13	people have brown hair
64	people have black hair

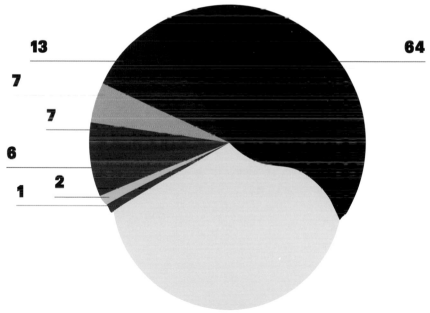

EDUCATION

LITERACY

83   people are able to read and write

17   people are unable to read and write

17

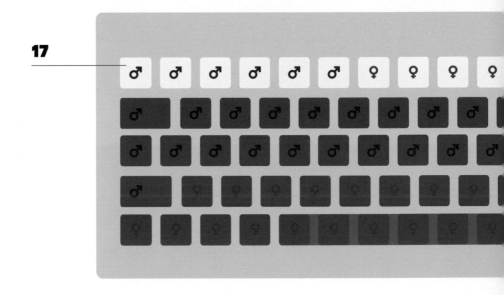

By gender

44 males and **39** females are able to read and write

6 males and **11** females are unable to read and write

83

PRIMARY SCHOOL

38   males have a primary school education

36   females have a primary school education

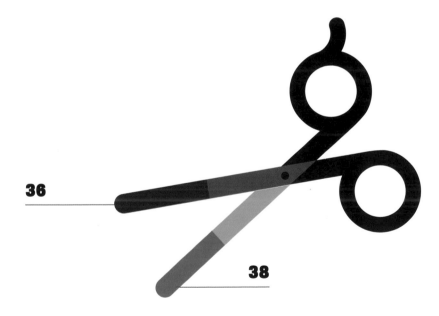

36

38

SECONDARY SCHOOL

33 males have a secondary school education

31 females have a secondary school education

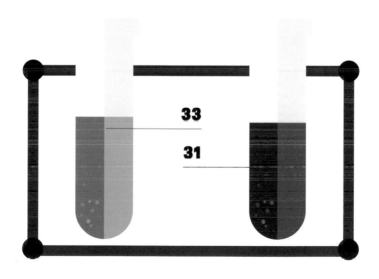

UNIVERSITY

7   people have a university degree

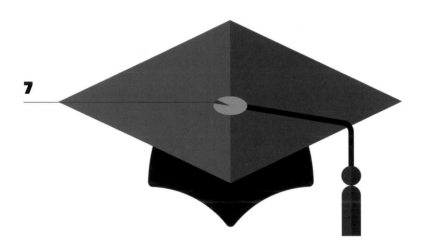

7

POST-GRADUATE

1 If the world were a village of 500 people, person would hold a PhD

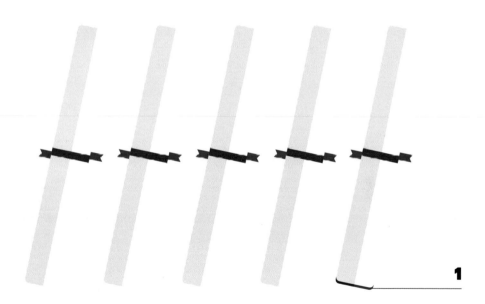

1

WEALTH

WEALTH

1   person owns 48% of the world's wealth

99   people share the remaining 52%

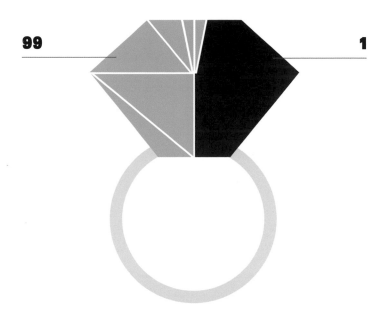

99   **1**

POVERTY

48   people live on less than US$2.50 per day

52   people live on more than US$2.50 per day

48   52

OCCUPATION

66   adults are employed

8   adults are unemployed

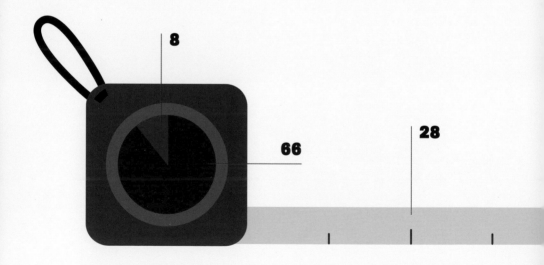

8

66

28

Of the employed

28 work in services

24 work in agriculture

14 work in industry

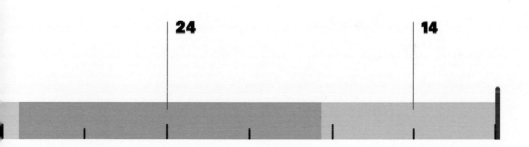

24   **14**

TRANSPORTATION

11   people own a car

36   people own a bicycle

11

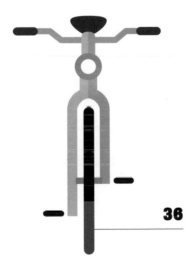

36

GOVERNMENT

REFUGEES

1   person is a refugee

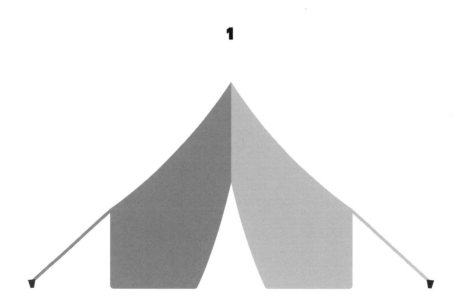

TRUST IN GOVERNMENT

50   people trust their government

50   people don't trust their government

50

50

FREEDOM OF SPEECH

52   people have freedom of speech

48   people don't have freedom of speech

LIVING IN FEAR

80   people don't live in fear

20   people live in fear

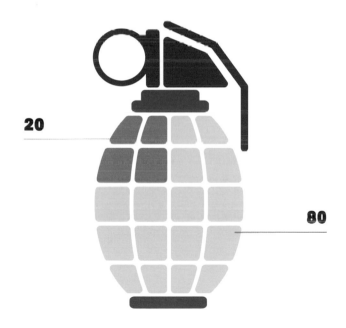

20

80

HEALTH

DISABILITY

85   people have no disability

15   people have a disability

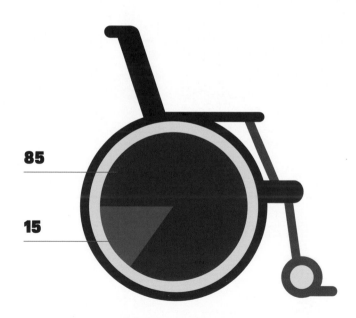

85

15

PHOBIAS

97   people have no phobias

3   people have phobias

VISION

96   people have regular sight

3   people are sight impaired

1   person is blind

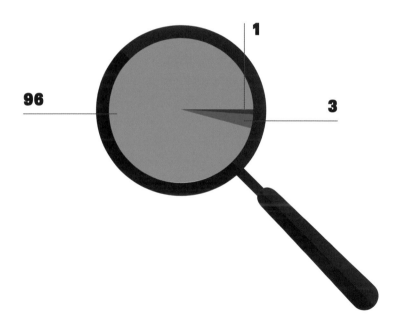

HEARING

95	people have regular hearing
4	people are hearing impaired
1	person is deaf

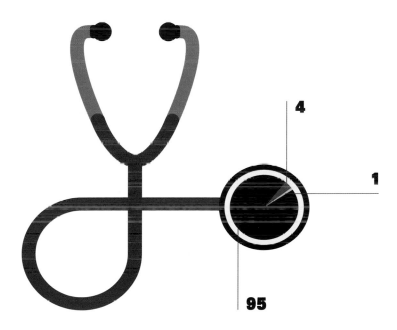

OBESITY/STARVATION

63	people are of normal weight
12	people are overweight
9	people are obese
15	people are undernourished
1	person is starving

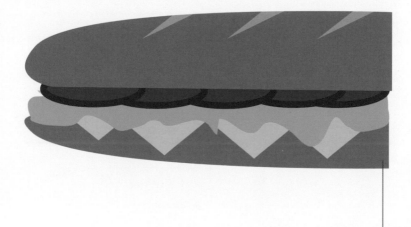

63

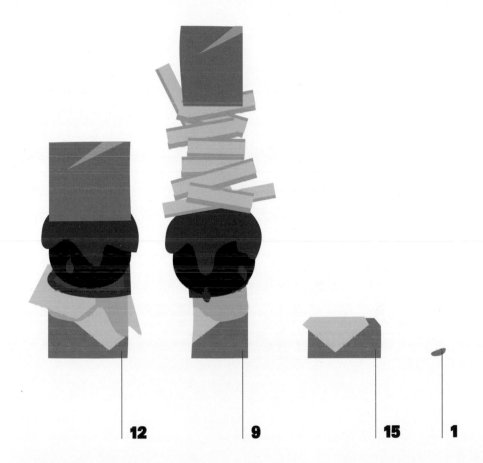

12   **9**   **15**   **1**

DEPRESSION

95   people don't have depression

5   people live with depression

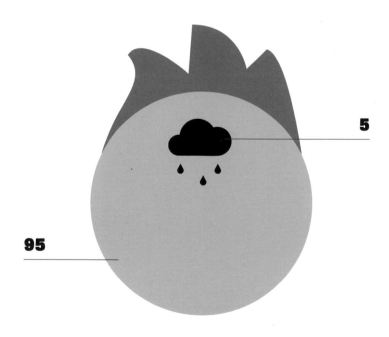

DIABETES IN ADULTS

91   adults don't have diabetes

9   adults live with diabetes

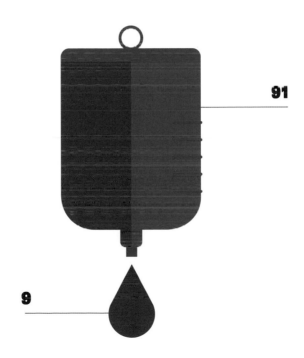

91

9

HIV

1   person is HIV-positive

1

MALARIA

97   people don't have malaria

3   people live with malaria

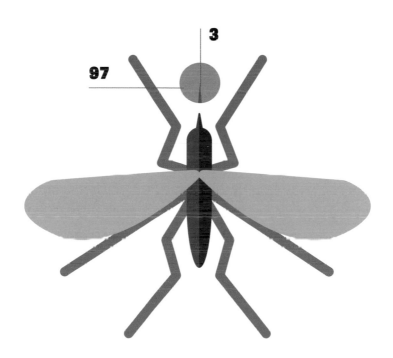

SMOKING

86   people are non-smokers

14   people smoke

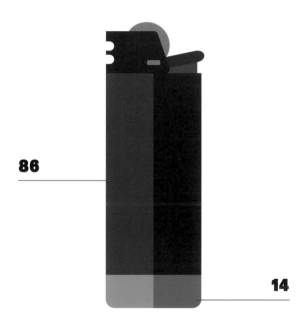

86

14

ALCOHOL DEPENDENCY

95 people don't have alcohol dependency

5 people have alcohol dependency

5

95

VEGETARIANISM

95   people consume meat

5   people are vegetarian

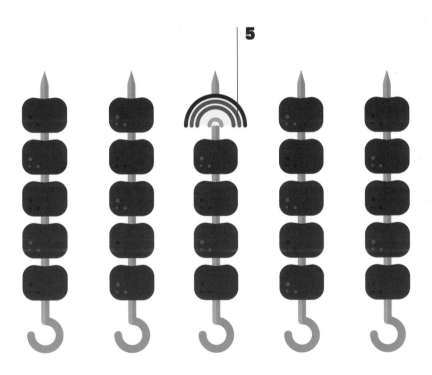

STAPLES

50   people eat rice every day

50

ACCESS

ACCESS TO TOILET FACILITIES

86   people have access to toilet facilities

14   people have no access

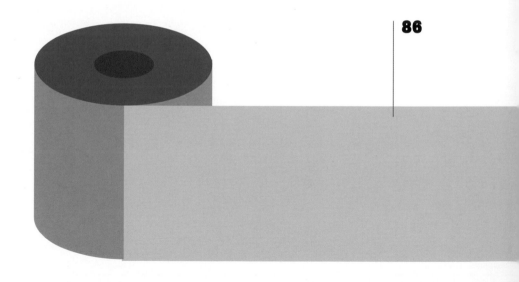

86

14

ACCESS TO WATER

87   people have access to safe drinking water

13   people have no access

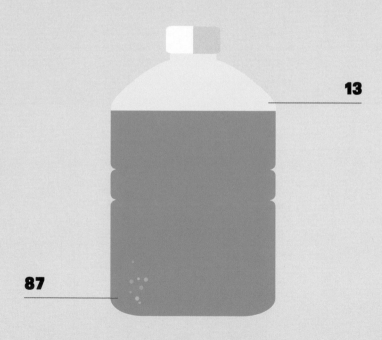

ACCESS TO ELECTRICITY

78   people have some access to electricity

22   people have no access

FAMILY PLANNING

3   women have no access to family planning

FERTILITY RATE

50   women will give birth to 117 children, a fertility rate of 2.33

2.33

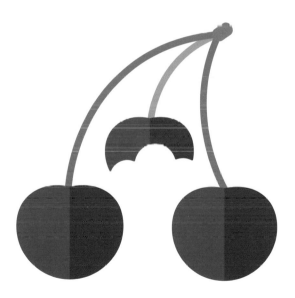

COOKING

40   people cook using solid fuels – wood, crop waste, charcoal, coal and dung – in open fires

60   people cook with gas or electric

60

40

SOCIAL MEDIA

21   people have a Facebook account

5   people have a Twitter account

4   people have an Instagram account

21

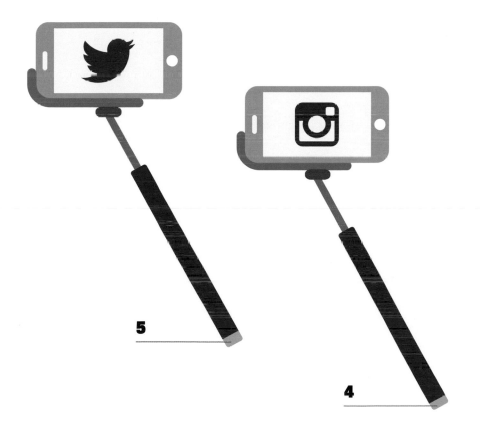

5

4

TELEPHONES

70   people have at least one mobile phone
(of which there are more than 100)

15   people have a fixed-line phone

OF THE MOBILE PHONES

45 are smartphones: 9 Samsung, 6 Apple iPhones,

4 Huawei, 3 Xiaomi; 23 are other brands

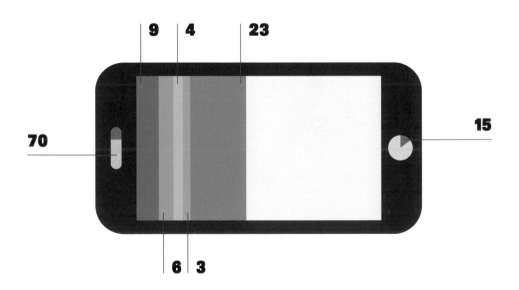

INTERNET

40 people have access to the internet
9 of whom are from China
4 of whom are from the US
3 of whom are from India

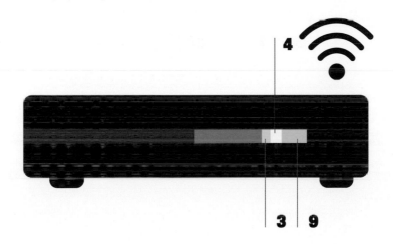

About the illustrator

Aileen Lord loves creating stories through images and works across a range of creative disciplines. She lives in Melbourne with an irrational collection of sneakers and magazines. *The World as 100 People* is her first illustrated title.

www.aileenlord.com   @aileenlord

Published in 2016 by Smith Street Books

Melbourne | Australia

smithstreetbooks.com

ISBN: 978-1-925418-08-8

Note: every effort has been made to ensure the accuracy of the statistics and the illustrations used in this book. In some instances, data collected varies – and sometimes contradicts itself – depending on source material. However, we have tried to rely on the most trustworthy sources available at the time of publishing.

CIP data is available from the National Library of Australia.

Publisher: Paul McNally
Design and Illustration: Aileen Lord
Editorial Consultants: Lucy Heaver & Hannah Koelmeyer, Tusk studio
Introductory text: Lucy Heaver, Tusk studio

Printed & bound in China by C&C Offset Printing Co., Ltd.

Book 7

10 9 8 7 6 5 4 3 2